C000024298

Sheffield

a pocket miscellany

Jonathen Skews

The History Press

First published 2012

The History Press
The Mill, Brimscombe Port
Stroud, Gloucestershire, GL5 2QG
www.thehistorypress.co.uk

British Library Cataloguing in Publication Data.
A catalogue record for this book is available from the British Library.

ISBN 978 0 7524 6624 8

Typesetting and origination by The History Press
Manufacturing managed by Jellyfish Print Solutions Ltd
Printed in Great Britain

Sheffield City Council Coat of Arms

DEO ADJUVANTE LABOR PROFICIT

First granted to the borough council in 1875. On the left is Viking god Thor, and on the right the Greco-Roman god Vulcan. Both represent the area's metal-working past.

The motto states, 'With God's help our labour is successful'.

Contents

Sheffield

The name of the city derives from the River Sheaf, running through the city.

In the Domesday Book (1086), the city is referred to twice by name – firstly as 'Escafeld' and then as 'Scafeld'. The name of the river itself means to 'divide' or 'separate'. The Sheffield area was a boundary between Anglo-Saxon kingdoms.

The Field or Feld part refers to open ground or perhaps a forest clearing.

Both parts are from Old English.

Grid Reference

Grid reference: SK 35714 87496

X: 435714
Y: 387496
Latitude: 53.38
Longitude: -1.46

Shares latitude with:
Liverpool
Dublin, Ireland
Edmonton, Canada
Magnitogorsk, Russia
Szczecin, Poland
Krumhorn, Netherlands

Shares longitude with:
North Shields
Southampton
Nantes, France
Tlemchen, Algeria
Kumasi, Ghana

Districts of Sheffield

Abbeydale
Local fact: Home of the Argentinean and Swiss teams during the 1966 World Cup.
Located here: Abbeydale Industrial Hamlet, Abbeydale Park.

Attercliffe
Local fact: Its name really does mean 'at a cliff'.
Located here: Sheffield Arena, Don Valley Stadium.

Beauchief
Local fact: Home of an abbey first built in 1183.
Located here: Beauchief Abbey, Beauchief Hall.

Bradfield
Local fact: There is man-made mound here of unknown origin, though possibly Saxon or Norman.
Located here: Edge of the Peak District National Park.

Brightside
Local fact: Vickers foundry was one of the main targets of Nazi bombing.
Located here: Industry.

Burngreave
Local fact: A hoard of Roman coins were discovered here in 1900.
Located here: Mostly just houses.

Carbrook
Local fact: Sheffield Co-op was founded here in 1868.
Located here: Centretainment Leisure Park.

Chapeltown
Local fact: Churchill Tanks were constructed here in the Second World War.
Located here: Mostly just houses.

Crookes
Local fact: Bronze-Age burial and metal-working was discovered here.
Located here: Mostly just houses.

Crosspool

Local fact: Sandygate Road is the oldest football ground in the world.

Located here: Tapton Hill Transmitter.

Darnall

Local fact: Charles I's executioner is rumoured to be from Darnall.

Located here: Mostly just houses.

Dore

Local fact: Egbert of Wessex briefly unified England here in AD 829.

Located here: Mostly just expensive houses.

Ecclesfield

Local fact: First founded during the Roman era.

Located here: Ecclesfield Park.

Grenoside

Local fact: The Grenoside Sword Dance dates back to the eighteenth century.

Located here: Mostly just houses.

Halfway

Local fact: Halfway is the end of the line for Supertram, how ironic!

Located here: Mostly just houses.

Handsworth

Local fact: It's had many famous residents from Sean Bean to Benjamin Huntsman.

Located here: The twelfth-century St Mary's Church.

Heeley

Local fact: Home to Sheffield United and Bramall Lane.

Located here: Heeley City Farm, Bramall Lane Stadium.

Highfield

Local fact: Sheffield's unofficial Chinatown.

Located here: Lots of restaurants and takeaways.

KING ECGBERT OF WESSEX
LED HIS ARMY TO DORE
IN THE YEAR A·D 829
AGAINST KING EANRED
OF NORTHUMBRIA
BY WHOSE
SUBMISSION
KING ECGBERT
BECAME FIRST
OVERLORD
OF ALL
ENGLAND

High Green
Local fact: Home to the Arctic Monkeys.
Located here: Wharncliffe Crags.

Hillsborough
Local fact: Home of Sheffield Wednesday.
Located here: Hillsborough Stadium, Hillsborough Arena.

Hyde Park
Local fact: The first Yorkshire *v.* Lancashire cricket match took place here.
Located here: Park Hill flats.

Loxley
Local fact: Robin Hood is supposedly from Loxley. The locals WILL inform you of this.
Located here: Mostly just houses.

Meersbrook
Local fact: Formerly the boundary between Northumbrian and Mercian kingdoms.
Located here: Meersbrook Park, Bishop's House.

Nether Edge
Local fact: The area is modelled after Boston, Massachusetts.
Located here: Sheffield Botanical Gardens, Lantern Theatre.

Owlerton
Local fact: Gives Sheffield Wednesday their nickname, the Owls.
Located here: Owlerton Stadium.

Tinsley
Local fact: Former site of the famous cooling towers.
Located here: Meadowhall shopping centre.

Walkley
Local fact: A nineteenth-century rumour was that a volcano would erupt here!
Located here: Mostly just houses.

Sheffield has many other districts:

Beighton
Ecclesall
Fulwood
Gleadless
Greenhill
Hemsworth
Longley
Malin Bridge
Manor
Middlewood
Millhouses
Mosborough
Neepsend
Norton
Oughtibridge
Pitsmoor
Ranmoor
Ringinglow
Sharrow
Stocksbridge
Totley
Wadsley
Wadsley Bridge
Wisewood
Woodhouse
Woodseats
Worrall

Sheffield's Twins

Seven different cities around the world are now twinned with Sheffield!

Anshan, People's Republic of China
One of the great steel and iron producing cities in the world. At the height of the industrial revolution, Sheffield produced around 20,000 tonnes of steel annually. Today, Anshan manages around 20 million tonnes each year.

Bochum, Germany
Set within Germany's industrial Ruhr region, Bochum is a city with a past in steel and coal.

Donetsk, Ukraine
Another steel- and coal-producing city. This one was founded by a Welshman called John Hughes in the 1870s. During the communist era, the city was named 'Stalin'.

Estelí, Nicaragua
A city with an industrial past, but not in steel or coal. Following the Cuban revolution, cigar makers moved here, and it is now an award-winning cigar-making city.

Kawasaki, Japan
In the 1920 Japanese census, the town had a population of 21,391. Today it has a population of 1.3 million and is the ninth largest city in Japan.

Kitwe, Zambia
Copper, not coal, is the substance mined here. The town was founded when a railway line was built in the area by the Cecil Rhodes' company.

Pittsburgh, United States
Pittsburgh shares its nickname 'the Steel City' with Sheffield. No prizes for guessing the main industry here.

Sheffield around the World

Sheffield, Tasmania
Edward Curr was manager of the wool-manufacturing Van Diemen's Land company. In 1859, Curr named a new town in Tasmania after his home city of Sheffield.

Sheffield, Illinois
American railroad magnates Henry Farnam and Joseph E. Sheffield founded a town in 1852. Local myth has it that the two tossed a coin to decide who it would be named after.

Sheffield, Alabama
This small town is home to a recording studio used over the years by such artists as Bob Dylan, Lynyrd Skynyrd, the Rolling Stones, Simon & Garfunkle and Elton John.

There are other, smaller Sheffield's in:
New Zealand
Iowa
Massachusetts
Ohio
Pennsylvania
Vermont
As well as in our very own Cornwall

Top Ten Strangest Street Names

1. Letsby Avenue (South Yorkshire Police have the last laugh with this recent addition to the map. It would be criminal not to put this at number one)

2. Stalker Lees Road

3. Sackville Road (not in fact the location of the job centre)

4. Moonshine Lane

5. Jaunty Way

6. Cyclops Street

7. Balaclava Road

8. Bacon Lane

9. Carsick Hill Road

10. Dead Man's Hole Lane

Timeline

Roman fort built at Templeborough. (The name comes from the mistaken belief that the fort was a temple.)

Norman Conquest.

During the Second Barons' War, Sheffield is destroyed.

Earliest surviving part of Sheffield Cathedral constructed.

Earliest evidence of human occupation in Sheffield towards the very end of the Ice Age.

A little Anglo-Saxon hamlet called Sheffield is established.

Domesday Book mentions Sheffield.

Great famine hits Europe, Sheffield starves.

c.11,000 BC   AD 70   6th-9thC.   1066   1086   1266   1315   1430

500BC   AD 410   Late 9th C.   1069   1215   1296   1348

Iron Age Brigantes tribe build hill forts in the area, which can still be seen today.

Late ninth century – Viking settlers establish many of the outlying regions of Sheffield.

Magna Carta signed.

The Black Death arrives in England and spreads to Yorkshire.

Last Roman soldiers leave Britain, signalling the start of the Dark Ages.

Harrying of the North. The area is almost completely wiped out by William's forces.

Kind Edward grants a license for a market to be held in Sheffield.

24

Sheffield Castle demolished by Parliamentarian forces.

Sheffield and Rotherham Railway opens.

Great Sheffield Flood: 270 people are killed as Dale Dyke Dam breaks.

Start of the English Civil War. Locals seize Sheffield Castle in the name of Parliament.

Thomas Boulsover invents Sheffield Plate, lowering the cost of manufacturing many items.

Henry Bessemer patents his Bessemer Process, allowing mass production of steel.

German zeppelin bombs Sheffield during the First World War.

1642   1648   1743   1838   1855   1864   1916

1570   1643   1740   1819   1844   1857   1912   1940

Royalist forces take Sheffield.

Opening of the Sheffield Canal.

Sheffield FC is formed, the world's first football club.

The Luftwaffe bombs Sheffield during the Second World War.

Friedrich Engels visits Sheffield to see the conditions of workers. Later he would write the Communist Manifesto with Karl Marx.

Mary Queen of Scots imprisoned in Sheffield Castle.

Benjamin Huntsman invents crucible steel.

Harry Brearley invents stainless steel.

Weather Records

Weston Park weather station has been recording data since 1883. Here are the records:

Hottest summer month in Sheffield history
July 2006 – 20.05 Celsius average.

Coldest summer month in Sheffield history
June 1916 – a chilly 11.55 Celsius.

Hottest winter month in Sheffield history
November 1994 – 9.35 Celsius. Not much need for sun tan lotion though!

Coldest winter month in Sheffield history
February 1947 – minus 2.05 Celsius. Even less need for sun tan lotion.

Sunniest month in Sheffield history
July 2006 – 290.8 hours of sun in total. Okay NOW get the lotion.

Rainiest month in Sheffield history
June 2007 – 285.6mm in total. The result of all this was a large-scale flood as the Rivers Don and Sheaf burst their banks.

Biggest change in weather
In 1921, Sheffield folk were in for quite a shock when, between October and November, the average temperature plummeted by over 8 degrees. Come May 1922, though, the city was in for a reward, as temperatures went up by almost 8 degrees. The weather can't make up its mind, can it?

Demographics

In 1801, the population of Sheffield made up 0.7% of the total English population.

Between then and 2001, this changed to 1.04%. Sheffield's rapid growth is plain to see. The population more than doubled between 1801 and 1841, from 60,000 to 134,000 people. It doubled again between 1841 and 1881.

The population today stands at over 547,000 people.

There are a few thousand more female residents than male residents, making up 50.13% overall.

We have a very diverse modern Sheffield, which even has its own unofficial Chinatown (Highfield). People from all over the Commonwealth and beyond have settled in the area, with a particularly large Jamaican and British Asian population.

White British	83%
Mixed Race	2%
Asian	7%
Black	2%
Chinese	1%
Other	4%

Religion in the city is just as diverse, with both a large mosque and cathedral.

Christian	69%
Muslim	4.6%
Hindu	0.3%
No religion	18%

Demographics Continued

There is a clear gender imbalance in the over 60s. Women tend to live longer in general.

From the 2001 census we learn the following about the way people in Sheffield live today:

Single	34%
Married	48%
Divorced	10%
Widowed	9%
Household without car	36%
One car or van	43%
Two or more	22%
One person household	32%
Married couple	34%
Cohabiting Couple	9%
Lone parent household	9%
Other	16%

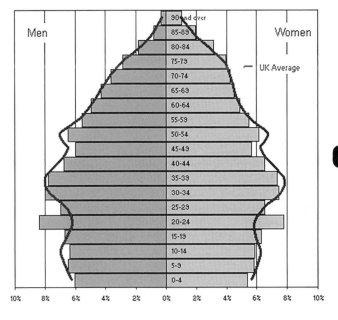

Men

Women

— UK Average

| 90 and over |
| 85-89 |
| 80-84 |
| 75-79 |
| 70-74 |
| 65-69 |
| 60-64 |
| 55-59 |
| 50-54 |
| 45-49 |
| 40-44 |
| 35-39 |
| 30-34 |
| 25-29 |
| 20-24 |
| 15-19 |
| 10-14 |
| 5-9 |
| 0-4 |

10%   8%   6%   4%   2%   0%   2%   4%   6%   8%   10%

Quotations

'What a beautiful place Sheffield would be, if Sheffield were not there!'
(The opinion of one Walter White, back in 1861)

'Everything is mean, petty, and narrow in the extreme. What a contrast to Leeds!'

(Anthony Mundella, MP for Sheffield in 1871. One wonders how he managed to get re-elected until his death in 1897!)

'It could justly claim to be called the ugliest town in the Old World: its inhabitants, who want it to be pre-eminent in everything, very likely make that claim for it … And the stench! If at rare moments you stop smelling sulphur it is because you have begun smelling gas.'
(George Orwell)

Geography

Sheffield is said to be built on seven hills, just like Rome. Its location makes it ideal for metal working and the industry that thrived here, with hills and rivers in all the right places.

George Orwell did not like the city, and the stereotype of Sheffield as a grey industrial place may have some grounding in reality. But doubters are in for a surprise. Sheffield has over two million trees – more than any other city in the UK. That's about four times the number of people in the city.

Naming the seven hills may be a challenge for any of the residents, but the city is certainly a hilly one, a fact anyone carrying heavy bags of shopping home can attest to.

The lowest point in the city lies at just 29m above sea level, at Blackburn Meadows. The highest point, at 548m, is the aptly named High Stones!

Steepest Hills

1. Hagg Hill

2. Blake Street

3. Wellfield Road

4. Jenkin Road

5. Fir Street

With a gradient of around 17%, Hagg Hill is the steepest in Sheffield.

Blake Street, meanwhile, is the people's champion. Folk tales about rolling cars and bob sledding may or may not be true. Certainly over the years, many have regretted 'popping for a swift pint' to the pub which sits at the very top of the hill.

Buildings

The architecture of Sheffield ranges from the city's gothic cathedral, Art Deco Central Library and Neo-Classical City Hall, to modern-day marvels such as the car park known affectionately as 'the cheese grater' on Arundel Gate.

As you would expect in such a large city, Sheffield has quite a selection of interesting and iconic buildings, including:

Park Hill
Possibly the most controversial construction in the city – people either love it or hate it. These 'streets in the sky' were seen as the future of housing, and were part of a new brutalist design ethic. Described as 'an eyesore' by many, they have been listed since 1998, despite being unoccupied.

Roxy Disco
The logo may be gone, but the building itself remains. In its 1980s heyday, this club was the height of cool in South Yorkshire, with locals wearing questionable outfits to dance to The Human League.

Tinsley Towers
Travelling along the M1, you knew you were home when you saw the salt and pepper pot cooling towers. Alas they are no more; no doubt thousands of people missing the junction they want as a result.

The Egg Box
A building that looked like an egg box! Everyone hated it, but now it's gone they miss it; an icon of its time.

Sandygate Road
The oldest football ground in the world, built in 1804. Forget Wembley and the Macarenathe; this is the real home of football.

Tallest Buildings

On the hurting-your-neck-while-trying-to-see-the-top-ometer, two buildings in Sheffield stand head and shoulders above the rest:

Arts Tower

78 metres doesn't sound like much, but imagine forty people stacked on top of each other.

St Paul's Tower

The tallest building in Sheffield, at 101 metres. In total, St Paul's Tower cost £40 million to build, which is roughly £400,000 per metre. The tallest building in the world, the Burj Khalifa, stands at 828m and cost $15 billion, roughly £11 million per metre.

Companies

The people of Sheffield are an industrious bunch and have started companies in many a field through the years.

Henderson's
Some people will tell you its Worcestershire Sauce, some ketchup or even vinegar. But everyone in Sheffield is in agreement; the best thing to have with your cheese on toast is Henderson's Relish, made in Sheffield for over 100 years.

Thorntons
Joseph Thornton opened his first chocolate shop in Sheffield in 1911, and over 100 years later the brand is as strong as ever.

Pinewood Studios
Charles Boot of Sheffield built Pinewood Studios in Buckinghamshire way back in 1934. Since then some of the nation's favourite films and characters, from *James Bond* and *Sherlock Holmes* to the *Carry On* franchise, have been created here.

Local Dialect

It may sound like a foreign language, but people in Sheffield are actually speaking English, or at least their own version. Here is a guide to some of the more common phrases you may hear.

Dee-Dar – people in nearby Rotherham and Barnsley say tha and thee, but in Sheffield, people pronounce it dee and dar. Hence locals are called dee-dars

Na then – greetings friend

Na then – let's get on with this

Eyup – greetings friend

Eyup – look out

Eyup – an exclamation of surprise

Eyup – practically anything you want it to mean

Spice – sweets

I'll go to foot of our stairs – I don't believe it

Nesh – unable to withstand cold weather easily

Sithee – farewell

Sithee – listen to me

Breadcake – bap, bun, roll, everyone has their own word!

Mardy – stroppy

Got monk on – very stroppy

Aye – yes

Oh aye – most certainly yes

This only gives you a minor grasp of the lingo however. Try and decipher this sentence, with a few new words added:

Eyup na then sithee lad, tha's gorra get some snap darn thee befoor 'avin spice; and dunt get monk on wi me neither!

Music

Pulp
What Morrissey is to Manchester, Jarvis Cocker is to Sheffield. When Blur and Oasis were competing with each other in the 1990s, everyone in Sheffield knew Pulp were the best.

Arctic Monkeys
With the fastest selling debut album in British history, these lads have become one of the best-loved bands of the modern era. Of course ask any Sheffield local and they will have 'seen 'em down the Leadmill before they were popular.'

The Human League
One of the most important British music acts of the 1980s. 20 million records sold worldwide.

ABC
1980s synthpop pioneers, with hits such as 'Poison Arrow' and 'The Look of Love'.

Joe Cocker
No relation to Jarvis, but nevertheless ranked as one of the 100 greatest singers of all time by *Rolling Stone* magazine.

Def Leppard
One of the top selling artists of all time, with a staggering 65 million albums sold. Terrible haircuts though.

Football

We already know about Sheffield FC, the world's oldest football club, and Sandygate Road, the world's oldest football ground.

Before any single code was employed, the Sheffield Rules were the ones used in this area. They were the first to introduce free kicks, throw-ins and corner kicks. As well as this, the rules introduced crossbars and heading the ball. The rules went on to influence football's development nationally.

The Steel City Derby is well known for its passionate fans, but Hallam and Sheffield FC have been playing each other since 1860, the world's oldest derby. Hallam FC won the first ever football tournament, the Youdan Cup, in 1867.

Modern football in Sheffield revolves around Sheffield Wednesday and Sheffield United. The rivalry is intense, with many a family falling out after one team has lost the derby.

Sheffield United have won the FA Cup four times to Wednesday's three. Wednesday have won the Football League more though, with four titles overall. United fans will tell you that they won the league in '98, but what they really mean is 1898.

A city with such a long footballing history surely must have a few good players? Well, one stands out more than the others; a pivotal part of the World Cup winning team of '66, Gordon Banks.

Sporting Heroes

Gordon Banks

Considered to be one of the greatest goalkeepers of all time. An England World Cup hero in 1966. He is arguably even more well known for his appearance in the 1970 World Cup, where he performed the 'greatest save of all time' against the renowned Pelé.

Jessica Ennis

A European and World Championship heptathlon gold medallist. She suffered heartbreak in 2008 after injury prevented her going to the Olympic Games in Beijing, but has since recovered to become one of the nation's best-known athletes.

Naseem Hamed

A former world featherweight champion. Outside of the ring he has proven a controversial character, but his performances and flamboyant style won many fans over a relatively short but successful career.

Howard Wilkinson

One of the few footballers to have played for both Sheffield United and Wednesday. He is currently the last English manager to have won the league title and has had two short spells in charge of the national team.

Harry Wright

Almost completely unknown in Britain, or even Sheffield, he is however one of the most influential figures in the history of baseball. After emigrating to the United States, he helped to set up the first professional team, the Cincinnati Red Stockings in 1869.

Sports Teams

Apart from Sheffield United, Sheffield Wednesday, the historic Hallam FC and Sheffield FC, the city does host one more club; Rotherham United are temporarily based at the Don Valley Stadium while their new stadium is being built.

Yorkshire County Cricket Club
Formed in Sheffield in 1863, the most successful team in English cricketing history. They were originally based at Bramall Lane, but haven't played in Sheffield since 1996.

Sheffield Steelers
Ice hockey may not be the most popular sport in Britain, but the Steelers regularly get thousands of spectators at the Motorpoint Arena. The team has won plenty of trophies, winning the Elite League as recently as 2011.

Sheffield Sharks
Alliteration beats geography as landlocked Sheffield names its basketball team after a fish. The Sharks have been pretty successful through the years, winning the league title four times in twenty years.

Sheffield Eagles
Rugby League has traditionally been more popular in the north of England, and Sheffield is no exception. Just as things were going well in the Super League, a disastrous merger with Huddersfield Giants ended up with a loss of top league status.

Cinema

In recent years, a few popular films have been set in Sheffield.

The Full Monty (1997)
One of the top British comedies of the 1990s. A group of men form a raunchy dance act after losing their jobs at a local steel mill. They do in fact leave their hats on, much to the pleasure of their audience.

Threads (1984)
At the height of the Cold War, the Soviet Union launches a nuclear strike against Sheffield. Presumably they have seen the fighting threat of drunken Sheffield men on a Friday night and fear total annihilation. This film follows the aftermath of the attack.

When Saturday Comes (1996)
Local lad Sean Bean takes his last chance to become a Sheffield United footballer. Basically *Rocky* but with gritty Northern folk and footballs.

Four Lions (2010)
Chris Morris, of *Brass Eye* fame, directed this black comedy about a group of would-be terrorists from Sheffield. Cue controversial jihad related high-jinx.

No look at Sheffield's film history would be complete without mention of the following two actors.

Sean Bean
As Sharpe, he bashed the French, in *When Saturday Comes* he beat Man United, as Aragorn in *The Lord of the Rings* he defeated the forces of evil. He's gone undercover in *James Bond*, become Ulysses in *Troy* and now stars in HBO's new hit series *Game of Thrones*. Is there anything he can't do?

Michael Palin
Part of the greatest comedy act in history, *Monty Python*, he enjoyed an extremely successful career in such films as *Life of Brian*. That would be enough for most people, but Palin has since gone on to travel the world in his BBC documentaries, making him one of the most popular television presenters around today.

People's Republic of South Yorkshire

Sheffield has a long history of trade unionism, socialism and lots of other 'isms'.

In the 1980s, Sheffield City Council was under Labour Party control, with local man David Blunkett at the helm. The council was to adopt a number of policies which led to the satirical name 'People's Republic of South Yorkshire'.

Three stand out the most:

1. Flying the Red Flag on 1 May. This date is known worldwide as Labour Day or Workers Day. The red flag is a symbol of socialism. At the height of the Cold War, flying a symbol synonymous with the Soviet Union was quite a shock.

2. Donetsk is a city in Ukraine. During the 1980s it was part of the Soviet Union. Sheffield City Council twinned the two cities.

3. Sheffield was declared a nuclear free zone. It was not alone in this as around 200 local authorities in the UK adopted the same idea. No doubt the film *Threads* had something to do with it.

Robin Hood

Nottinghamshire has attempted to steal this outlaw. In 2004, Yorkshire and Nottinghamshire MPs even tried to settle the matter in parliament! But Sheffield has the strongest claim to him.

Robin of Locksley, supposedly born in Loxley to the north-west of the city, is connected with this region in all the earliest tales.

There are wells and streams all around named after Robin and his Merry Men and even Doncaster Sheffield Airport is called Robin Hood Airport.

Whether the man existed or not is a matter of great debate. If he did exist it is likely that he was born in Loxley (an old cottage there was even claimed to be his exact birthplace), but carried out most of his adventures across South Yorkshire and Nottinghamshire. Forests at the time covered more ground, and the wooded area of Loxley joined with the famous Sherwood Forest. The evil Sherriff of Nottingham's purview extended across large swathes of land, very close to Sheffield in fact.

Sheffield Universities

The two Sheffield universities have a total of around 58,000 students. If we assume they all live in Sheffield, this makes up more than 10% of the total population!

University of Sheffield
Founded: Sheffield School of Medicine in 1828, awarded university status in 1905
Students: *c.* 25,000

Sheffield Hallam University
Founded: Sheffield School of Design in 1843, awarded university status in 1992
Students: *c.* 33,000

The University of Sheffield is the most prestigious of the two city universities; consistently ranked as one of the best universities in the UK. Five Nobel Prize winners are associated with it. They are:

Nobel Prize for Physiology and Medicine
Professor Howard Florey (1945)
Professor Hans Krebs (1953)
Robert J. Roberts (1993)

Nobel Prize in Chemistry
Professor George Porter (1967)
Sir Harry Kroto (1996)

Economy

At a total of over £9 billion, if Sheffield were a country, its economy would be larger than that of many real countries. The Sheffield economy is roughly equal in size to Macedonia. Per head, roughly equivalent to South Korea.

Over the last thirty years, Sheffield has been transformed from an industrial powerhouse to a service-based economy.

Job Type	Percentage in 2008
Manufacturing	10.9
Construction	4.2
Services	84.5
Distribution, hotels & restaurants	22
Transport & communications	5.1
Finance, IT, other business activities	19.6
Public admin, education & health	33.4
Other services	4.3
Full-time	66.8
Part-time	33.2

In 1995, twice as many people worked in manufacturing!

The economy in Sheffield has traditionally been built around the manufacture of steel and other metal products.

The truth is that while fewer employees work in the steel industry, modern technology and processes mean that the city is making more steel now than ever before. These metals are often of a very high quality, used in aerospace and other high-tech applications.

The Steel City lives on!

Theatres

Theatre has been considered throughout history as one of the hallmarks of civilisation; even the Ancient Greeks loved a good play.

No surprise then that such civilised people as those in Sheffield have a large cinema complex, the largest in the UK bar the West End no less.

Lyceum Theatre
Situated inside a marvellous Edwardian building, the Lyceum has hosted many a performance since it was first built in 1897. For a while the theatre was used as a bingo hall.

The Crucible
Where the real drama takes place. Every year, for over thirty years, thousands of people descend on the Crucible to watch the World Snooker Championships. The Crucible was refurbished recently at a cost of around £15 million. Roughly 1,000 people can be seated at any one time.

The Studio
Opened in 1971, it can accomodate 400 people in total. Situated in the same building as the Crucible.

Festivals

Doc/Fest
One of the main international documentary film festivals –
held in Sheffield since 1994.

Grin Up North
Started in 2010, all the best British comedians come to
Sheffield for a whole month.

Tramlines
Forget Glastonbury or Woodstock, Tramlines is the king.
Top UK acts from many music genres take over the city for
a weekend. Most of the events are free to attend.

There are plenty of other annual festivals too, including:
Art Sheffield
Sheffield Poetry Festival
Fright Night – Britain's biggest Halloween party

Museums and Galleries

Millennium Gallery
Hosting everything from modern art to Sheffield's metalworking past. New exhibitions are hosted here every few months.

Weston Park Museum
Promising the 'Story of Sheffield from ancient history to the present day' and delivering much more. A great natural history area and 5 hectares of greenery.

Graves Art Gallery
Named after John George Graves, former Lord Mayor of Sheffield and the man who made it possible with his investment. Located in the same building as the central library, it even hosts works by such artists as Pablo Picasso.

Bishops' House
Built way back in 1500 for two bishops, John and Geoffrey Blythe (even though they never lived here the name stuck). One of the oldest buildings in Sheffield and one of only three timber structures surviving in the city.

Kelham Island Museum
The story of Sheffield's industrial past, on a 900-year-old man-made island!

Abbeydale Industrial Hamlet
A working museum exhibiting all manner of industrial techniques. Metal-working has taken place on this site as far back as the 1300s.

Things to Do and See in Sheffield

Magna
Located in a steelworks just across the Rotherham border, this science adventure centre is sure to keep the whole family entertained.

Ski Village
The largest artificial ski centre in Europe.

Ponds Forge
Apart from an Olympic-size swimming pool, there are plenty of other sporting and fitness activities to keep you occupied here.

Botanical Gardens
5,000 different types of plants across 19 acres.

Peak District
The second most visited national park in the world, and right on Sheffield's doorstep.

Winter Garden/Peace Gardens/Millennium Gallery
All sorts of attractions rolled into one. Exotic plants and the perfect place to eat your lunch.

Meadowhall
280 stores across two floors and 1.5 million square feet. As well as all that there is a food court and a cinema. Retail heaven.

The Moor
One of Sheffield's busiest shopping streets and home to Atkinson's department store.

Fargate
The main high street in Sheffield, all the latest fashion trends can be found here.

Castle Market
Located in the city centre, with over 200 stalls. People come from miles around to buy fresh fish, meat, fruit and veg here.

Criminals

Spence Broughton

Stand and deliver; your money or your life! No, not Adam Ant, but Spence Broughton (*c.* 1746 – 14 April 1792), a notorious highwayman.

In 1791, Broughton and an accomplice held up the Sheffield and Rotherham mail. They committed two more robberies in England in the same year before they were caught. All very exciting, but not why Broughton is famous.

As punishment for his crimes, Broughton was executed by hanging in 1792. Afterwards his body was gibbeted at Attercliffe Common, between Sheffield and Rotherham, where the first robbery took place.

Here his body remained until 1827 – thirty-five years after it was first placed there. 40,000 locals turned up to see this spectacle on the first day, and it remained a popular attraction until its removal, when the new land owner grew sick of people wandering across his property to view the corpse! Nearby Broughton Lane is named after Spence.

Charles Peace

Films and books have enhanced the legend of Charles Peace. His father was a lion tamer; it was never going to be a straightforward life for Charles.

In his early years, Peace was in and out of prison for burglary and petty crimes. During one of these sentences he attempted a daring prison escape.

After periods where he worked as a picture framer, he went to America, where he returned to burglary. During one attempt, he shot a policeman dead. Another man was blamed for this and sentenced to death, later commuted to life imprisonment.

For some years, Peace had been bothering a woman who spurned his attentions. In 1876, during an altercation, Peace shot the woman's husband dead. He now had a price on his head and went on the run, travelling around the country. He managed to evade arrest for two years, committing theft wherever he went, but was captured in 1878. At his trial he was sentenced to death. But one more remarkable act was to take place. Peace admitted and proved his own guilt, releasing the man previously thought to have killed the police officer.

. The Life of .

CHARLES PEACE

FROM THE ONLY EXISTING PHOTOGRAPH OF THE MALEFACTOR IN THE POSSESSION OF THE POLICE

"Famous Crimes" Edition.

Crime Statistics

Crime	Crime rate (per 1,000 residents) 2008/9	National Average, England and Wales
Burglary	15.9	11
Criminal Damage	23.6	17
Drug Offences	3.4	4
Fraud and forgery	2.8	3
Offences against vehicles	19.1	11
Other offences	1.2	1
Other theft offences	22.7	20
Robbery	1.5	1
Sexual offences	0.7	1
Violence against the person	16.1	16

Media

BBC Radio Sheffield
On air since 1967, only the second local radio station in the UK.

Sheffield Telegraph
Founded in 1855
Website: www.sheffield telegraph.co.uk

Sheffield Star
Founded in 1887
Website: www.star.co.uk

Distance from...

Place	Distance (in miles)
Ayers Rock, Northern Territory	9,333
Brussels, Belgium	303.5
Centre of the Earth	3,959
Death Valley	5,135
Eiffel Tower, Paris	352.5
Frankfurt, Germany	488.7
Guernsey, Channel Islands	488.7
Hong Kong	5,959
Isle of Man	139.5
Jerusalem	2,346.3
The Kremlin, Moscow	1,552.8
London Eye	141.2
The Moon (average)	238,857
The North Pole	2,530.2
Osaka, Japan	5,829.1
The Panama Canal	5,231.3
Queenstown, South Africa	11,706.6
Reykjavik, Iceland	1,034
The Sun (average)	92,955,807.3
The Taj Mahal	4,311.7
Ulaanbaatar	4,283.1
Vatican City	1,020.9
Washington DC	3,572.9
Xanthi, Greece	1,483.8
Yellowstone National Park	4,468.9
Zurich	725.8

Parks

Sheffield has thirteen city parks, twenty district parks and fifty local parks, making a total of eighty-three parks in the city!

The thirteen city parks are:

Concord Park

Cholera Monument Grounds

Endcliffe Park/Porter Valley Parks

Ecclesall Woods

Firth Park

Graves Park & Animal Farm

Hillsborough Park & Walled Garden

Millhouses Park

Norfolk Heritage Park

Peace Gardens

Rivelin Valley Park

Sheffield Botanical Gardens

Weston Park

Legends

Sheffield has its own Walk of Fame, just like Hollywood!
This is based outside the Town Hall in the city centre.
The people honoured so far are:

Gordon Banks – England World Cup goalkeeper

Sean Bean – Internationally famous actor

Joe Cocker – Singer (no relation to Jarvis)

Sebastian Coe – Lord, Olympian and head of the 2012
Olympic Organising Committee

Derek Dooley – Footballer with Sheffield Wednesday,
whose short career was sadly cut short due to his leg being
amputated following a serious fracture in his last match for
the club

Jessica Ennis – Gold-medal winning athlete

Professor Barry Hancock – Much respected cancer expert

Brendan Ingle – Boxing manager and coach

Def Leppard – Rock band, with millions of records sold

David Mellor – Highly esteemed designer

Michael Palin – Monty Python member and world traveller

Joe Scarborough – Artist

Helen Sharman – First Briton in space

Joe Simpson – Mountaineer and writer

Michael Vaughan – England cricket captain

Clinton Woods – Champion boxer

Sheffield Steel

Metal-working has long been an important part of life in Sheffield. For hundreds of years iron was the main output, but Sheffield is known throughout the world as the Steel City. Here is the story of three men who built the Steel City.

Benjamin Huntsman

Huntsman was the son of German immigrants, born in Lincolnshire in 1704.

Initially a clockmaker, he discovered a new method of steel production after moving to Sheffield. Crucible steel was born, allowing increased production and kick-starting the Industrial Revolution; but Sheffield was not interested. Amazingly, Sheffield cutlers decided that the steel was no good for what they wanted, and continued to import steel from Germany. Meanwhile, Huntsman started exporting his steel to France, whose cutlers then imported vast quantities of cutlery, out-competing Sheffield! Eventually the Sheffield cutlers backed down. Benjamin Huntsman, however, did not patent his process and his idea was stolen by a man named Walker, who sneaked into the factory disguised as a beggar.

Henry Bessemer

The Bessemer process allowed even greater quantities of steel to be produced at a low price. Yet again, nobody was interested in his idea, but this time, when he brought it to Sheffield, people did take notice. Mass production of steel began here. The company he set up managed to undercut the competition by a large amount and really set the wheels in motion for Sheffield's Steel City status.

Harry Brearley

The only one of our three pioneers actually born in Sheffield. Endless experimentation in the lab led him to create and patent Stainless Steel. Since then his steel can be found across the world, perhaps most famously in the New York Chrysler building.

Nearby Towns

Rotherham
In recent years, Sheffield and Rotherham have begun to merge into one large mass.

Rotherham also has a steel making and industrial past. Gordon Banks is from Sheffield, while another of England's great goalkeepers, David Seaman, hails from Rotherham. William Hague is also a Rotherham man, although proud Labour supporters in Rotherham will tell you that the Chuckle Brothers are their most revered sons.

Barnsley
Barnsley coal powered the Sheffield furnaces. This town lies to the north of Sheffield and its most important resident was Sheffield-born Joseph Locke, the great railway and engineering pioneer.

Doncaster
A Roman fort called Danum quickly rose to become a large town. Doncaster lies to the east of Sheffield and is perhaps best known for Conisbrough Castle, the setting for Sir Walter Scott's novel *Ivanhoe*.

Chesterfield
To the south of Sheffield lies Chesterfield, home to the famous crooked spire. Shoddy workmanship is the most common explanation, but the truth is that nobody really knows why it is so twisted.

Bakewell
At first glance, the map looks pretty empty between Sheffield and Greater Manchester. To the south-west of Sheffield, however, a string of villages have popped up. Chatsworth and its Great House is one of the most well known, but Bakewell and its tarts win the nation's hearts.

What People Love about Sheffield ...

The Peak District. In Sheffield you are never more than a few minutes walk from something green, but it's the Peak District that really captures people's imagination.

Friendly locals. Need directions? In Sheffield not only will people not swear at you, but they will actually tell you the right route!

The famous village feel. For a big city, Sheffield has the atmosphere of many small, interconnected villages (well, it pretty much is).

All the different events and museums/galleries. Best of all, many of them are free.

The sheer variety. Sheffield is a city of contrasts, and not just because of the hills! You can be standing outside an old industrial building one minute, only to turn a corner and find an ultra-modern masterpiece.

Sheffield never stands still for long. There is always something happening or something new to see and do.

... and what People Hate about Sheffield

Too many traffic lights and a confusing one-way system. Driving through the city needs to be carefully planned weeks in advance.

People with clipboards conducting surveys in the city centre. Like vultures, it is said they can detect prey from up to half a mile away.

Sheffield United or Sheffield Wednesday, depending on your allegiance. It is widely agreed by Sheffielders, however, that Rotherham United and Barnsley are both scum.

Sheffield folk love a bit of shopping. The only problem is they all go at once. Meadowhall has been dubbed 'Meadow Hell' by locals. Getting past thousands of tourists to see the Mona Lisa at the Louvre in Paris is child's play compared to buying new socks at Marks & Spencer on a Saturday afternoon.

Park Hill Estate. Revered by many, hated by an equal amount. If you want to start a bar-room brawl in Sheffield, mention the flats.

Students. Sheffield may be a student city, but it won't take long for you to find someone who thinks students are 'noisy beggars' who have 'daft haircuts'.

All the hills. Great when cycling down them, not so much on the way back up.

Transport

Road

As you would expect, Sheffield does in fact have a road network. The city is connected to the North and South via the M1, which skirts past the Rotherham border. Sheffield has a free – yes free – city centre bus service.

Rail

Sheffield has had its own railway station since 1838, the earliest days of railway transport. Nowadays, the rather splendid Pond Street station is able to take you anywhere you need to go.

Air

Sheffield formerly had a city airport at Tinsley. Today, Sheffield is served by the Doncaster-Sheffield Robin Hood Airport. A marvellous name; flights are available to such distant destinations as Barbados.

Canal

The Sheffield Canal was opened in 1819. Should you wish to travel via this method, the option is still available.

Tram

Pretty much all the major cities in Europe have access to the above means of transport. What sets Sheffield apart though is its Supertram! For just a few pounds the tram can take you all over the city in a jiffy.

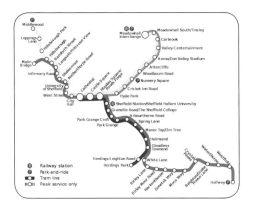

Sheffield Online

There are lots of sites on the World Wide Web where you can find out about Sheffield, including:

www.sheffield.gov.uk
The home of Sheffield City Council, with information on every topic imaginable.

www.sheffieldforum.co.uk
A very popular forum covering all things Sheffield.

www.sheffieldtheatres.co.uk
The best place to book tickets and find out what shows are on.

www.welcometosheffield.co.uk
Sheffield tourist information.

www.peakdistrict.gov.uk
www.visitpeakdistrict.com
Unsurprisingly, the best Peak District information online.

Blue Plaques

Blue plaques around the country mark the birthplaces of British heroes and well-known figures of all kinds. Sheffield, however, currently holds just two.

One commemorates the home of **Sir Henry Coward**, Doctor of Music and leader of the Sheffield Philharmonic Chorus, which is still active today.

The other commemorates the **Thornton family**, chocolatiers extraordinaire, who also have an ongoing influence in Sheffield life.

Not to fret, however, discussions are underway about more plaques, and the city does have Sheffield Legends – a Walk of Fame located outside the Town Hall which, like the Hollywood version, honours famous people from or connected to the city.

Ghosts

In a city with such a long history, it's no surprise that there are dozens of reportedly haunted buildings and sightings of apparitions. Several pubs claim to be the 'most haunted in Sheffield', although how one would establish such a fact is rather puzzling.

Stocksbridge Bypass

If you are driving along at night and spot a group of children playing in the road, don't worry, they are most likely not real children in danger, but simply evil ghost children hell-bent on destroying the world. You may also spot a monk or any number of other ghosts and ghoulies. This is the most famous haunted location in Sheffield, with hundreds of reported sightings, even by the police. Keep your car doors locked!

Botanical Gardens

Watch out for ghost dogs! If you should be bitten by said dog, report immediately to your local exorcist for treatment.

Bunting Nook

If you are eloping with a lady (or boy) friend, while on horseback, maybe avoid Bunting Nook. The last couple to do so still haunt the area after falling and breaking their necks.

UFOs

If you manage to avoid the ghosts while in Sheffield, you still need to be on the alert, as several sightings of UFOs have been reported!

One of the most common occurrences in Sheffield is a floating orange glow. Many people in Sheffield have seen this and suspected something strange. The truth is that the orange UFOs are indeed from another place . . . they are Chinese lanterns. The lanterns were first created in ancient China and are often lit on special occasions.

Not all sightings can be explained, however. One incident has become infamous and nobody knows what exactly happened. In the last few hours of 24 March 1997, many observers were awaiting the arrival of a visitor from space – the Hale-Bopp comet.

What they saw instead was a low-flying aircraft, which appeared to crash in the Peak District. South Yorkshire police took many calls reporting an object covered in bright lights, followed by a large flash or explosion, sightings of smoke, and even military aircraft.

A full-scale search was launched immediately, but nothing at all was found, and no aircraft were reported as missing.

Was it an alien spaceship and a government cover-up? Was it a secret military test gone wrong? Could it be a chunk of Hale-Bopp? Nobody knows. The authorities, including the South Yorkshire police, have no explanation for the occurrence and no idea what could have caused it. Or is that just what they want us to think?

Statues

Pan – Botanical Gardens
Greek God and 'Spirit of the woods'.

Queen Victoria – Endcliffe Park
'Erected by citizens of Sheffield in memory of a great queen'.

Vulcan – On top of the Town Hall building
Roman God and blacksmith.

King Edward VII – Fitzalan Square
Funded by the people of Sheffield following his death.

Ebenezer Elliot – Weston Park
A poet instrumental in the repeal of the Corn Laws, a great political debate of his day.

Steelworkers – Meadowhall Shopping Centre
A well-known meeting point controversially moved outside the building.

The Sheffield City Battalion

Pals Battalions were units of men from specific towns who all signed up to fight alongside each other in the trenches during the First World War. The Sheffield City Battalion was one of these.

At the outbreak of the war, roughly 1,000 Sheffield men from all walks of life quickly enlisted. They spent most of 1915 training in England, before being sent to guard the Suez Canal in Egypt.

Soon after, however, the unit was sent to France, in preparation for an Allied attack.

The Steel City boys were to hold the far left of the line at a village called Serre. The offensive was the horrific Battle of the Somme. Within minutes, the battalion was cut to shreds by enemy machineguns. After just two days, the remnants of the battalion were withdrawn from the front line. They had lost over half of their strength, 513 dead in total, most of whom were killed within minutes.

Hundreds more men were killed and wounded throughout the remainder of the war, as the battalion struggled on.

All of these men are commemorated in a memorial park in Serre.

Born in Sheffield

Many famous people are associated with Sheffield, but who was born here?

Thomas Boulsover – cutler and inventor – 1705

John Roebuck – chemist – 1718

Francis Leggatt Chantrey – sculptor – 1781

Samuel Earnshaw – polymath – 1805

Joseph Locke – railway pioneer – 1805

Thomas Creswick – painter – 1811

Sir William Sterndale Bennett – composer – 1816

John Fowler – civil engineer – 1817

John Christopher Cutler – second Governor of Utah – 1846

Leonard Cockayne – botanist – 1855

Charles Harding Firth – historian – 1857

Robert Hadfield – metallurgist – 1858

Robert Murray Gilchrist – author – 1867

Joseph Thornton – chocolatier – 1870

Harry Brearley – Stainless Steel inventor – 1871

James Stuart Blackton – silent film producer – 1875

Fred Varley – painter – 1881

Arthur Lismer – painter – 1885

Derek Bailey – jazz guitarist – 1930

David Mellor – designer – 1930

Malcolm Bradbury – author – 1932

Roy Hattersley – Labour politician – 1932

Brian Glover – wrestler and actor – 1934

Judy Parfitt – actress – 1935

A.S. Byatt – Booker Prize-winning author – 1936

Gordon Banks – World Cup-winning goalkeeper – 1937

Joe Scarborough – artist – 1938

Michael Palin – comedian – 1943

Howard Wilkinson – football manager – 1943

Joe Cocker – singer – 1944

David Blunkett – Labour politician – 1947

Paul Carrack – musician – 1951

Sean Bean – actor – 1959

Graham Fellows (aka John Shuttleworth) – comedian – 1959

Steve Clark – Def Leppard guitarist – 1960

Jamie Reeves – World's Strongest Man winner – 1962

Jarvis Cocker – Pulp frontman – 1963

Helen Sharman – astronaut – 1963

Dominic Wet – actor – 1969

Mark Gasser – concert pianist – 1972

Naseem Hamed – boxer – 1974

Jessica Ennis – Athletics champion – 1986

Alex Turner – the Arctic Monkeys frontman – 1986

Sheffield City Council

William Jeffcock
The very first Mayor of Sheffield was William Jeffcock, in 1843. Relatively little is known of his life, although it is certainly undeniable he had extraordinary sideburns.

Henry Fitzalan-Howard
In 1897, the Mayor of Sheffield was transformed into the Lord Mayor, the role which still exists today. The first to hold this post was Henry Fitzalan-Howard, the Duke of Norfolk and one of the most powerful men in the country at the time. The Duke is known as a great philanthropist and contributed greatly to Sheffield throughout his life.

Sheffield Council has twenty-eight wards, each of which elects three councillors. Overall control has been invested in the Labour Party throughout most of the last forty years, although Liberal Democrats have gained some power in recent years. At the time of writing, Conservatives hold absolutely no seats on the council, reflecting the industrial roots of the city.

Sheffield Elections

The Reform Act of 1832 gave Sheffield its own representation in parliament. Two men became the first Members of Parliament for Sheffield in that year.

John Parker

A member of the Whig Party. Parker was an important figure in the creation of a Sheffield constituency and was rewarded by voters with twenty years in parliament, representing Sheffield.

James Silk Buckingham

A member of the Radicals, Buckingham certainly led a unique life. As a thirteen-year-old boy he was aboard a Royal Navy ship when it was captured by the French, and was kept as a prisoner of war. He later travelled throughout the Levant and Arabian Peninsula, then on to India. Here he set up a newspaper, which led to him being expelled from the country by the East India Company, who did not appreciate his criticism. This was all before his election in Sheffield!

Today Sheffield has five constituencies, four of which are Labour strongholds. Sheffield Hallam is one of the richest areas of the country and has seen strong support for the Conservative and Liberal Democrat parties.

Unusual Modes of Transport

At the beginning of the twentieth century, motorcars and trucks were still few and far between. Horses were employed as a mode of transport and for agricultural use too; however, at the outbreak of the First World War, thousands of horses were needed on the frontline.

Thomas Ward Ltd was a scrap metal trading company based in Sheffield (the company still exists today) which had a bit of a problem when many of its horses were sent to the Front. When 'Sedgewick's Menagerie', a travelling animal show, visited the area, it was decided the company would borrow an elephant.

Lizzie the Indian elephant helped Ward's to transport all manner of goods around the city, doing the work of several horses with ease! Imagine the look on people's faces when they saw an elephant wandering around the streets of industrial Sheffield. The firm started something of a trend, with camels also being employed in the city.

Many stories about Lizzie exist, some more dubious than others. Over the years, Lizzie (supposedly) played in goal during the Steel City Derby, ate a schoolboy's cap, broke a window to steal a pie, and took part in all manner of other adventures.

Demographics II

By British standards, Sheffield is a fairly large city. But how does it compare to the world's most extreme cities?

Population of Sheffield (2010): 546,986
Population of Shanghai (2010): 17,836,133

Sheffield: 370 km^2
New York: 8,683 km^2

Sheffield population density: 3,950 people per km^2
Mumbai population density: 29,650 people per km^2

The Sheffield Stock Exchange

The City of London today holds a monopoly on trading and other financial activity. However, in its heyday Sheffield had its very own Stock Exchange.

This exchange was first created in 1844, at the height of the railway boom, and later dealt with coal and steel shares, amongst other commodities. The exchange existed until 1965, when it merged into the Northern Stock Exchange.

For most of its life, the Sheffield Stock Exchange was based in, you guessed it, Commercial Street.

Green Sheffield

Sheffield may be the greenest city in the UK purely in number of trees and parks, but how about it's carbon footprint?

Calculations by the Stockholm Environmental Institute show that in 2005, Sheffield's total CO_2 emissions added up to a staggering 5,798,361 tonnes. This is the equivalent of emissions from 13,484,560 barrels of oil or 1,136,934 cars for a year.

So what are we doing about it? Well, quite a lot. Various schemes to cut the city's carbon footprint are in place. The most interesting of these are six Sheffield City Council vans, which are run on gas created by raw sewage!

Sheffield Panorama

Page